DayOne

HELP!

I'M DROWNING IN DEBT

Dr. John Temple

Consulting Editor: Dr. Paul Tautges

© Day One Publications 2011

First printed 2011

ISBN 978-1-84625-249-5

All Scripture quotations, unless stated otherwise, are from the English Standard Version, Crossway, 2001.

Published by Day One Publications
Ryelands Road, Leominster, HR6 8NZ

TEL 01568 613 740 FAX 01568 611 473

email—sales@dayone.co.uk

UK web site—www.dayone.co.uk

USA web site—www.dayonebookstore.com

All rights reserved

No part of this publication may be reproduced, or stored in a retrieval system, or transmitted, in any form or by any means, mechanical, electronic, photocopying, recording or otherwise, without the prior permission of Day One Publications.

Designed by **documen**
Printed by Orchard Press (Cheltenham) Ltd

Contents

	Introduction	5
1	Debt Everywhere	8
2	Common Causes of Debt	15
3	The Bible on Debt	27
4	Practical Solutions	34
	Conclusion	58
	Personal Application Projects	59
	Where Can I Get Further Help?	62

Introduction

Some years ago, a postgraduate student won a scholarship to fund his studies in another country. The home country was not aware of the cost of living in his new country, so the scholarship awarded was wholly inadequate. As a foreigner, his wife was unable to take a job, so the couple took in a boarder to help spread their accommodation costs. The student also took on two teaching jobs, despite putting his registration as a full-time student at risk. They lived frugally, but none of this averted the need to borrow money to survive. Eventually, the student completed his studies and returned home. Setting up a home, buying a car and feeding a wife and, by now, two children was not easy. There was no possibility of paying off the loan and, now that the studies were complete, the interest started to pile up. The only solution was to borrow more money to pay for the interest!

Does this sound familiar? It is very familiar to me because I was that postgraduate student. In short, *my family was drowning in debt.*

Some debt may be unavoidable and even justifiable. The situation that we found ourselves in may have been such a case. The debt was incurred despite every attempt to avoid it, and we certainly kept it to a minimum. It was also incurred for a good cause—education—the outcome of which should have helped us repay it.

Maybe you are in a position similar to the one I faced. If you are concerned about debt—whether because you wish to reduce your own debt, you want to learn how to avoid it, or you want to help others who are sinking in debt—this booklet is for you.

Throughout the booklet I assume that you are a follower of Jesus Christ who wants to pursue the principles of finance set out in the Bible. But perhaps you are not a follower of Christ, and you wish to be one. When the apostle Paul was asked what a person had to do to be saved, his answer was,

> *Believe in the Lord Jesus, and you will be saved.*
>
> (Acts 16:31)

Introduction

It is impossible to believe in Jesus without believing what he came to do.

Our relationship with God is broken because we are sinners. Because God is holy, our sin requires punishment. But God loves sinners. Therefore, he sent his Son, the Lord Jesus, to take our place, taking the punishment due to us when he died on the cross. Three days later, Jesus rose from the grave as proof that he is who he said he was, and that the debt of man's sin had been fully paid. God now commands us as sinners to repent and believe in Christ. When we turn to Christ for our salvation, for the forgiveness of our sins, we are reconciled to God (Romans 5:10), and we begin a new life in which the Holy Spirit enables us to glorify God, even in the midst of the pressures of life—even along the long, hard road of getting out of debt.[1]

---

[1] To learn more concerning God's wonderful plan for our salvation, see the publication *How Can I Become a Christian?* listed at the end of this booklet under "Where Can I Get Further Help?"

Debt Everywhere

What are the reasons why so many today are calling out "Help!" as they drown in debt? I suggest the following as the most likely:

- "Justifiable debt" incurred in a good cause. Examples include a mortgage or payment for education, provided that the outcome of the training leads to a higher income. Another justifiable loan is one which increases our productivity and earning power, such as when a carpenter or plumber purchases power tools.

- Debt caused by rash or foolish decisions.

- Debt to fund living beyond our means. This and other foolish decisions are the most likely causes, so I expand on these causes below.

- Emergency debt. This may be caused by a

sudden illness, loss of a job, a natural disaster, and so on. If it is unavoidable, it is probably justifiable, but it remains a problem.

- Debt incurred to help someone else, perhaps a family member. This may also be justifiable, but it remains a problem.

Debt is a universal problem in our modern economic order, and one that is not restricted to individuals. Anyone who has lived through the financial crisis of 2008 onwards is aware of this. Government "cuts" to reduce public debt are major news items. These cuts will probably not be sufficient, resulting in a "solution" of only minimal cuts, increased taxation, and inflation. Strange though it may seem, inflation is actually considered a "solution." If there is anything positive about inflation, it is that all paper assets, *including debts*, diminish in their "real" value. A debt of $1000 (or £1000) incurred fifty years ago would have taken an entire year's income to settle, but settling it today would probably cost a single month's earnings. In fact, part of the present crisis was triggered by the *assumption* that inflation was a permanent feature of our economic order. Mortgages were granted on houses at a value *exceeding the purchase price*. Banks gambled on housing prices

Help! I'm Drowning in Debt

rising so that loans would be secured by a high-value property. However, the downside of inflation is that *all* paper assets, including money-in-the-bank, also diminish in real value.

The fact that interest rates are so central to our economic order demonstrates the importance of debt. The central banks (Federal Reserve in the USA and Bank of England in the UK) are required to regulate interest rates in order to control inflation. The theory is that a lower interest rate will encourage borrowing by consumers and producers, thereby generating growth. But growth tends to put pressure on the supply chain, inflating incomes and other production costs. Raising interest rates is supposed to control the appetite for *debt* by both private and business borrowers, thereby curbing growth and inflationary pressures. In reality, it does not always work because political and other pressures are exerted (such as the need to generate employment), so that the solution is to sweep the real problems under the carpet, print money, and create even more inflation.

Sadly, this debt-laden environment has rubbed off on many of us. The mere fact that you have read so far in this booklet probably indicates that you are concerned. We too easily succumb to the secular culture, living in the "counsel of the ungodly" (Psalm 1:1, KJV). We want whatever our hearts desire, not pausing to think whether or not we *need* such things, even less whether we can *afford* them. All too often the major concern is how *affordable* an item is, a euphemism for "What are the monthly payments?" The outcome is to drown in debt.

In 2009 the average private debt in the USA was $700,000 per family; in the UK it was £400,000. This has come about through unrestrained greed by consumers who wanted more and more material possessions, services, and leisure. It has come about through greedy bankers who were happy to provide loans to fulfill the greed of their customers and, in the process, earn for themselves ludicrous bonuses on the "paper profits" made on these loans. Indeed, greed has been encouraged by most Western governments.

Western economies are largely "consumer-led." This means that people are encouraged to spend, whether it is necessary or desirable. This expenditure creates "demand," which is provided by an ever-increasing workforce in order to fulfill these wants. The outcome is apparent economic growth, full employment, and "success" that is hailed by governments. This is despite the fact that they have created huge national debt, which future generations will have to repay, and have not truly solved key economic problems. Standards of living also increase due to the ever-increasing spiral of better products and more sophisticated services.

Let me be clear: there is nothing wrong with a rising standard of living, and all of these good items are given by "... God, who richly provides us with everything to enjoy" (1 Timothy 6:17). However, the context of this verse is important: it is not urging unrestrained *indulgence*. Rising living standards are legitimate if generated by improved technology or increased productivity *and if they can be paid for*. The reality, however, is that demand for all sorts of goods and services (many of them nonessential) increases through high-pressure advertising and incentives such as reductions in interest rates aimed at increased consumer spending.

What happens when consumers demand more than can be justified in terms of productivity or technological gains? "Real incomes" (i.e. after inflation) cannot rise fast enough to overcome the effects of inflation. Add this to the increasing desire to live a "better life," and people *live beyond their incomes* and are forced to borrow. Here are some examples.

Debt Everywhere

- Home mortgages which exceed the value of the properties, creating so-called "negative equity" or mortgages that are "under water"—an apt description because it causes families to drown in debt.
- Credit cards issued to all, with scant regard to the credit-worthiness of the customers, and permitting just 5 to 10 percent payment of the balance each month, creating ever-increasing debt.
- Loans to buy automobiles, audio/video equipment, and other luxury goods.

In short, *living in debt has become an acceptable way of life in our culture.* If this is based on greed or other sinful desires, it is sinful. Listen to James:

> You desire ... You ask and do not receive, because you ask wrongly, *to spend it on your passions.*
> (James 4:2–3, emphasis added)

I often encounter families who tell me that they are struggling financially. Below the surface they blame the recession, or unfairness by their employers, the

Help! I'm Drowning in Debt

government, or greedy big business, especially the banks! Their stories are similar: to make ends meet it becomes essential for the wife to work, for them to incur debt, and to curtail what they give to the Lord's work. This may be true, and I do sympathize with such families, but in many cases the real reasons are the ones that I have given above. For example, I recently saw a low-paid worker complain on TV that in these difficult times he did not have enough pocket money to enjoy his overseas vacation after paying for air tickets and hotel bills. These are the major cultural contributors to *family* economic woes, and they set the scene for a biblical consideration of how things *ought to be*.

At the heart of our secular culture is the desire for *instant gratification*. Consume and enjoy *now*! In common with our secular society, as Christians we can easily fall into the trap of believing that spending now is our entitlement. We do not want to save before we spend. The oft-repeated slogan of the debt-based consumer society is "Buy now, pay later."

Common Causes of Debt

We are immersed in a culture of secular thinking which is contrary to biblical standards. We therefore need to identify the underlying causes of debt and its remedies from a biblical standpoint. Setting aside for now what I earlier called "justifiable debt" (we will return to this later), the *moral* reason why many Christians get into debt is based on one or more of the following transgressions:

- Wrong priorities
- Idolatry
- Covetousness
- Lack of contentment
- Lack of self-control

15

The first two problems can be dealt with by considering this passage from Matthew 6:

> Do not lay up for yourselves treasures on earth, where moth and rust destroy and where thieves break in and steal, but lay up for yourselves treasures in heaven, where neither moth nor rust destroys and where thieves do not break in and steal. For where your treasure is, there your heart will be also ... No one can serve two masters, for either he will hate the one and love the other, or he will be devoted to the one and despise the other. You cannot serve God and money. Therefore I tell you, do not be anxious about your life, what you will eat or what you will drink, nor about your body, what you will put on. Is not life more than food, and the body more than clothing? Look at the birds of the air: they neither sow nor reap nor gather into barns, and yet your heavenly Father feeds them. Are you not of more value than they? ... And why are you anxious about clothing? Consider the lilies of the field, how they grow: they neither toil nor spin, yet I tell

> *you, even Solomon in all his glory was not arrayed like one of these. But if God so clothes the grass of the field, which today is alive and tomorrow is thrown into the oven, will he not much more clothe you, O you of little faith? Therefore do not be anxious, saying, "What shall we eat?" or "What shall we drink?" or "What shall we wear?" For the Gentiles seek after all these things, and your heavenly Father knows that you need them all. But seek first the kingdom of God and his righteousness, and all these things will be added to you.*
> (Matthew 6:19–21, 24–26, 28–33)

What do we learn from this passage as it applies to debt?

Priorities

Maybe our priorities are wrong. Jesus says, "Seek *first* the kingdom of God' (v. 33, emphasis added), implying that it is legitimate to seek something else. The second priority is "all these things," which "will be added to you." What things? He speaks of welfare, clothing, food, and drink (v. 25).

Help! I'm Drowning in Debt

He reminds us that the same God who gives us these things also provides food for the birds and magnificent colors for the flowers and the grasses of the field (v. 30). All creation tells not only of God's provision, but also of his extravagant goodness. Jesus says that the Gentiles "seek after all these things" (v. 32). In the parallel passage in Luke 12:30, Gentiles becomes "nations," and the modern equivalent could well be "secular society." Jesus is saying that they *concern* themselves with material goods, but *we* do not need to be "anxious" (v. 31), because God knows that we need "them all." What is implied in "them all"? Jesus says that the lilies surpass Solomon in all his glory for beauty. Surely this teaches that God will give us more than all that we *need* to exist. He means to do for us what he does for the lilies when he adds beauty. He will be extravagant in his blessings, whether they are spiritual or material. In 1 Timothy 6:17, Paul writes, "God ... richly provides us with everything to enjoy." Note the word "richly," meaning that his blessings are more than merely adequate. But there is a condition: seek him *first*. This has practical application in our giving, in the use of our time, and in our attitudes. This priority will definitely show up in our personal budgets.

Idolatry

The second problem is idolatry. Our desire for material goods or services is at loggerheads with our desire to worship God because we tend to worship money and material possessions. Jesus points out that we cannot "serve money" and God at the same time (v. 24). The two are mutually exclusive. The meaning of "serve" here is "worship." It is an attitude that signifies where our treasure lies. Jesus urges us not to lay up treasure here on earth, but in heaven (vv. 19–21).

We readily make God's blessings into idols. We tend to think of "idols" as carvings of wood or stone, but in our modern world an idol is anything that we put ahead of God. Consider what we value or deem "worthy," that is, *what we worship*. Jesus taught that, by comparison with our worship of God, we must hate our relatives and even our own lives (Luke 14:26). He was not suggesting that we stop loving and caring for our spouses, children, or even ourselves; that would be contrary to other Scriptures. No, it is that he condemns the tendency to *idolize* these people.

It is worth stopping here. Consider what things or activities are close to your heart. Is it sports, entertainment, food, travel, money, possessions, gadgets, status, security, and so on? My wife had a friend who had been a top athlete. Athletics consumed her life to the extent that, after she was converted, she realized that, like the rich young ruler who was told to sell all that he had, she had to give up her sport. There is nothing wrong with sport (the apostle Paul says it is beneficial to the body), but she had made an idol of it, so it had to go. Are the "things" which got you into debt coming before God in your life?

Covetousness

The third problem is covetousness. This is a direct breaking of the tenth commandment:

> You shall not covet your neighbor's house;
> you shall not covet your neighbor's wife,
> or his male servant, or his female servant,
> or his ox, or his donkey, or anything that is
> your neighbor's.
>
> (Exodus 20:17)

Today, covetousness is evident in our desire to "keep up with the Joneses." We desire to have all that our neighbors, work associates, or friends have. Or, more generally, *we simply covet in order to live as the rest of society lives*. Do we even stop to consider whether or not we really need any of the things and services that everyone else enjoys? I know of two families that have never owned a television and have done exceptionally well. I also know people (admittedly in the UK) who have never owned or even driven a car. All too often, the real reason why we want something is to conform to the standards of those around us. Yet Paul urged us,

> *Do not be conformed to this world, but be transformed by the renewal of your mind, that by testing you may discern what is the will of God, what is good and acceptable and perfect.*
>
> (Romans 12:2)

There may be nothing wrong with any of the things we want, but we are not to *covet* them. James goes further when he says,

> *You desire and do not have, so you murder. You covet and cannot obtain, so you fight and quarrel. You do not have, because you do not ask.*
>
> (James 4:2)

Contentment

The fourth problem is a lack of contentment, due to greed. We always want *more*. Consider these words:

> Now there is great gain in godliness with contentment, for we brought nothing into the world, and we cannot take anything out of the world. But if we have food and clothing, with these we will be content. But those who desire to be rich fall into temptation, into a snare, into many senseless and harmful desires that plunge people into ruin and destruction. For the love of money is a root of all kinds of evils. It is through this craving that some have wandered away from the faith and pierced themselves with many pangs. But as for you, O man of God, flee these things. Pursue righteousness, godliness, faith, love, steadfastness, gentleness ... As for the rich in this present age, charge them not to be haughty, nor to set their hopes on the uncertainty of riches, but on God, who richly provides us with everything to enjoy. They are to do good, to be rich in good

works, to be generous and ready to share, thus storing up treasure for themselves as a good foundation for the future ...
(1 Timothy 6:6–11, 17–19)

Again, the priority is "godliness," that is, seeking to be conformed to God's standards. In line with the passage from Matthew 6, we are encouraged to be *content* with food and clothing (v. 8), always remembering that it is God who provides us with these. Note that Paul uses the same language that Jesus used about laying up treasure in heaven. Paul is not denying the possibility of being rich on this earth—he addresses the rich with special instructions in verses 17 to 19. However, he warns those who are *desiring to be rich*—possibly those who are in debt—of temptations, snares (could he be thinking of debt?), and senseless and harmful desires which "plunge" them into death and destruction. The outcome can even be the wandering away from the faith.

Paul is positive about what we *ought* to be doing. There is "great gain in godliness with *contentment*" (v. 6, emphasis added). He writes, "Pursue righteousness, godliness, faith, love, steadfastness, gentleness" (v. 11). Here is the key. The more we pursue godly

Help! I'm Drowning in Debt

virtues, the less we will be *discontented*. Paul had learned to be content in all circumstances, *whether he had plenty or too little* (Philippians 4:11). True contentment lies in our relationship with God; we are meant to *enjoy him forever*.

I recently suggested to one of my younger grandchildren that he read the chapter on pocket money from my book *Family Money Matters*.[2] I pointed out that he might be entitled to more money if he studied my suggestions. He replied that he already received $5.50 per month, but he had calculated that he would be content if he got $8.50! Is that not true of all of us? Every time I added up my assets to determine whether my wife and I had enough to go on pension, I always came to the same conclusion: I needed a bit more!

The key issue is that the materialistic, market-driven world is bombarding us with messages to make us *discontented*. All advertising seeks to make us desire something *better*. We become *discontented* when our neighbors get new cars. We are *discontented* with a mundane holiday spent at home playing with the children when our friends are off to exotic places. The list is endless, because marketing professionals are out to lure us with messages of *discontentment*.

2 See section "Where Can I Get Further Help?" for details.

Common Causes of Debt

Recognize what they are doing and resist it, because it is evil.

> *Resist the devil, and he will flee from you.*
> *(James 4:7)*

Self-control

This is the fifth and final problem. Proverbs 25:28 says,

> *A man without self-control*
> *is like a city broken into and left without walls.*

How apt! Our lives are easily "broken into." Advertising is designed to break down our resistance and make us discontented. The root cause of lack of self-control is a lack of the indwelling Holy Spirit, because one of the gifts of the Spirit is self-control (Galatians 5:23). Thankfully, if we are truly believers in Christ, the Holy Spirit indwells us and empowers us to develop this necessary virtue.

These five manifestations of our sinful hearts remind us of our inherent sinfulness. But thanks be to God that he sent Jesus to fully pay our sin debt on the cross, so that we could be set free! Even though we may not be free of financial debt, we can be fully free from the debt of our sin. Are you trusting Jesus as your sin-bearer, as the one who paid your sin debt?

The Bible on Debt

Giving biblical financial advice would be easier if God prohibited debt, but he does not; by giving us instructions on debt he recognizes its reality in a fallen world. However, he made this promise to the people of Israel:

> And if you faithfully obey the voice of the LORD your God, being careful to do all his commandments that I command you today, the LORD your God will set you high above all the nations of the earth ... The LORD will open to you his good treasury, the heavens, to give the rain to your land in its season and to bless all the work of your hands. And *you shall lend to many nations, but you shall not borrow.*
>
> (Deuteronomy 28:1, 12)

Help! I'm Drowning in Debt

Although this promise was given to the Old Testament nation of Israel, it surely suggests two general principles: that observing God's laws leads to prosperity, and that being a "borrower" is not God's best for any believer, whether an Old Testament Israelite or a New Testament Christian (see also Proverbs 22:7).

Consider also the following instructions on debt:

- "You shall not charge interest on loans to your brother, interest on money, interest on food, interest on anything that is lent for interest. You may charge ... interest, but you may not charge your brother interest, that the LORD your God may bless you ..." (Deuteronomy 23:19–20). I believe this applies to Christians today.

- Debts were to be forgiven every seven years (Deuteronomy 15:1–11). I believe that this means that, if Christians do lend (or borrow) money today, they had better make the term reasonably short.

- "When you make your neighbor a loan of any sort, you shall not go into his house to collect his pledge. You shall stand outside, and the man to whom you make the loan shall bring the pledge out to you. And if he is a poor man, you shall not sleep in his pledge. You shall restore to him the pledge as the sun sets, that he may sleep in his cloak and bless you. And it shall be righteousness for you before the LORD your God" (Deuteronomy 24:10–13). This teaches that the lender must respect the borrower's dignity (that he or she is made in God's image), and that his or her warmth and comfort must not be taken away.

- It is a sin to borrow and not repay: "The wicked borrows but does not pay back, but the righteous is generous and gives" (Psalm 37:21). "It is better that you should not vow than that you should vow and not pay" (Ecclesiastes 5:5).

- Do not stand surety for a loan between two other parties. Note these verses from Proverbs: "Whoever puts up security for a stranger will surely suffer harm, but he who hates striking hands in pledge is secure" (Proverbs 11:15); "One who lacks sense gives a pledge and puts up security in the presence of his neighbor" (Proverbs 17:18); "Be not one of those who give pledges, who put up security for debts" (Proverbs 22:26).

- In the parable of the talents, Jesus seemed to approve of a bank paying interest on investments: "Then you ought to have invested my money with the bankers, and at my coming I should have received what was my own with interest" (Matthew 25:27). While the central message of that parable was not about profit nor interest, Jesus would hardly have used such an example if he disapproved of either.

We have seen how *spiritual* problems can lead us astray and result in wrong attitudes toward material possessions and services. How do we overcome these problems? The same way all spiritual problems are cured:

- Through a real work of the Holy Spirit in our lives. Paul assures us, "In any and every circumstance, I have learned the secret of facing plenty and hunger, abundance and need. *I can do all things through him who strengthens me*" (Philippians 4:12–13). We need to submit to Christ and trust him to help us fight the temptations around us.

- Using all the means of grace available: Bible study, prayer, fellowship, and self-control.

We may need to confess that we have gotten ourselves into financial difficulty because we succumbed to temptations or acted foolishly. Listen to the words of Solomon:

Trust in the LORD with all your heart,
  and do not lean on your own
    understanding.
In all your ways acknowledge him,
  and he will make straight your paths.
Be not wise in your own eyes;
  fear the LORD, and turn away from evil.
It will be healing to your flesh
  and refreshment to your bones.
Honor the LORD with your wealth
  and with the firstfruits of all your produce;
then your barns will be filled with plenty,
  and your vats will be bursting with wine.
My son, do not despise the LORD's discipline
  or be weary of his reproof,
for the LORD reproves him whom he loves,
  as a father the son in whom he delights.
                              (Proverbs 3:5–12)

This passage tells us how we should live: by trusting God's revelation and not relying on our own understanding, that is, not being self-reliant. How often do we make decisions and choices based on what we consider to be right, only to have the outcome later blow up in our faces? Solomon says, "Do not lean on your own understanding" (v. 5); "Be not wise in your own eyes" (v. 7). Every decision that we make should be made in prayer and after reading those portions of the Bible that may have a bearing on the issue (see above list). Part of true fellowship is to consult other Christians. Be humble, and acknowledge that you have neither all knowledge nor all wisdom.

- By checking our priorities. Have you been giving to the Lord's work? Solomon says, "Honor the LORD with your wealth and with the firstfruits of all your produce" (v. 9). This is accompanied by a promise: "then your barns will be filled"— that is, prosperity. If you are already in very serious debt and have no *income*, you may have to defer "normal" giving until you have an income again. We cannot give away other people's money. However, giving to the Lord is *not* related to our financial status but to our *incomes*. So long as you have an income, "tithe" it and God will honor you.

- By learning God's lessons. Sometimes our hardships, financial or otherwise, are corrections of the Lord and are intended to train us. The last couple of verses of the passage above assure us that this is a sure sign of God's love for us. Make sure you learn the lessons early.

Practical Solutions

We must always hold two key doctrines in balance: the sovereignty of God and the responsibility of man. In getting out of debt, we must work at it as if we had never prayed, but we must also pray and trust God for help as if we had never worked. It is important, therefore, to beware of self-sufficiency. Our pride may have gotten us into a financial mess as we failed to pray about important decisions or to consult trusted Christians, and pride may keep us from deliverance. I can best illustrate this from correspondence I received recently:

> "My wife and I have been drowning in debt for many years. As the Lord has convicted me ... I came to realize that one of my chief sins is self-sufficiency ... By not trusting in the Lord with all my heart (Proverbs 3:5-6)

> *during the early years of our marriage ... and the first ten years at our church, which was very small and unable to pay me a full salary (I worked many outside jobs), I believe borrowing became a way that 'I' could solve our problem ... Unfortunately, my pride led to bigger problems. Pride that says, 'I made this mess, I can clean it up,' or the pride that manifests itself in being silent about one's legitimate needs. I chose the 'drowning' metaphor because it fits how I have felt for a long time."*

Even though this family's debts were probably justifiable, the pastor's confession is that he tried to tackle the solution on his own and got into deeper trouble in the process. God has promised to supply all our needs. Let me illustrate how God helped my family in our early high-debt years (all glory to him).

After I completed my thesis in London, several months elapsed while the examiners studied it and compiled questions for an examination. Just as all our money ran out, a company gave me short-term consulting work, supplying all our needs. Then my employer in South Africa asked me to investigate

Help! I'm Drowning in Debt

some opportunities in the corresponding British industry, paying all our expenses, completely solving our support problem. We had one final need: to get back to South Africa. With perfect timing, the patent which I and my supervisors had taken out on my work was sold. My share turned out to be—you've guessed it—the exact amount that my wife and I and our young daughter needed to get home. God does supply our legitimate needs!

The problem of self-sufficiency is more of a danger to competent people who may cross the line from humble self-confidence to pride. Beware!

How did my family get out of our debt problem? I had a good job (my debt was for education), but my income was inadequate for debt reduction. We bought an old car. I made furniture, painted our new house myself, and we lived frugally. Then we started doing *extra work*. My wife gave mathematics lessons, and I worked after hours, designing houses and organizing builders. The key lesson was that we *worked*, using "saleable" skills to get out of debt.

The Bible lists four means of bringing in money: work; return on investment; inheritance; and gifts. No "get-rich-quick" schemes, no gimmicks, no gambling in any form. Short of a windfall from something like an inheritance, the only option for most of us is to work our way out of our problem. In a nutshell, we should keep cool heads, incur no new debts, increase our incomes, cut our costs, and pay off our debts in some logical order (more of this below).

Before we turn to some practical ways of reducing debt, we should understand that all expenditure can be divided into two classes: consumption and investment.

"Consumption expenditure" includes items which lose their value after use so that we can never get our money back. An example is food; we buy it, we eat it, and it is gone forever. Health care, clothing, travel, entertainment, holidays, and sport are further examples. If, however, we spend wisely, these services will be beneficial to us. Keep your consumption expenditure to a minimum and, as a rule, *never get into debt for any consumption item—not for a holiday, sport, entertainment, nor even for a wedding, or special anniversary party*.

On the other hand, "investment expenditure" becomes an "asset" which remains ours. If we so desire, we may get some of our money back if we sell the item. Sometimes a "service" is an investment; for example, building a house (a service) will produce an asset.

Help! I'm Drowning in Debt

There are two kinds of assets: those that appreciate or gain value in time, such as a good house, and those that depreciate or lose value, such as a car. Assets such as furniture depreciate so fast that they become consumption expenditure. A badly chosen property, or renovations to a property which do not enhance the resale value by at least what they cost, also tends toward consumption expenditure.

It is reasonable to get into debt on some assets (e.g. property), but borrowing for any *nonessential* assets cannot be justified. Examples include luxury items such as audio/video equipment, jewelry, watches, cameras, and phones. Cars are somewhere in between.

So, what are the practical ways for dealing with debt?

Statement of Assets and Liabilities

First, you need to know where you are at present, regardless of how you got there. You may have got into debt through foolish decisions or succumbing to the temptations listed earlier. If so, then you should repent and ask God for forgiveness. You must not panic, because, as we saw in Matthew 6, Jesus also commanded us, "Do not be anxious." Paul went further by saying,

> *The Lord is at hand; do not be anxious about anything, but in everything by prayer and supplication with thanksgiving let your requests be made known to God. And the peace of God, which surpasses all understanding, will guard your hearts and your minds in Christ Jesus.*
>
> (Philippians 4:5–7)

God's grace extends to our foolishness and *especially to our sins*. Our debt-related sins are painful because they affect us and our families directly. But we need to ask ourselves whether we have not perhaps committed a more serious sin. The greatest sin is not to believe that Jesus Christ died on the cross in our place in order that we might never bear the just punishment for our sins. If you have never trusted Jesus to forgive you for *all* your sins, now is the time to get that right before you tackle your debts. All that is required is that you believe and repent, that is, change the direction of your life and follow Jesus Christ, trusting him as your sin-bearer.

Now make a summary of your assets (what you own) and your liabilities (what you owe, your debts). This is a "Statement of Assets and Liabilities," but

Help! I'm Drowning in Debt

do not let jargon put you off. This is a biblical step. Note Proverbs 27:23–27:

> Know well the condition of your flocks,
>   and give attention to your herds ...
> the lambs will provide your clothing,
>   and the goats the price of a field.
> There will be enough goats' milk for your food,
>   for the food of your household
>   and maintenance for your girls.

How would the writer have phrased these words today? Perhaps "Know the state of your assets, your investments, your bank accounts ... They will provide income for your family ..." The Statement will list your assets (described as "investments") *less* your debts, yielding your *net assets*. If this is a large "plus," then you are actually well off, although you may still have too much debt. In this case the solution is simple: sell off some of your assets and pay off your debts.

But it is likely that this exercise will show that you are "drowning" because your *debts exceed your assets*. Technically, you may be bankrupt. You must look realistically at the size of your problem so that you can make the right choices to fix it. After all, you may well have gotten into the problem by making *wrong* choices. There is no point in getting it wrong again!

Family Budget

If you are drowning in debt, you must make a family budget to see where you are spending your money so that you can focus on the places where you can cut expenditure. Space does not permit me to set out family budgeting in detail here, but you can find assistance in the resources listed at the end of this booklet.

As you form your budget, divide items into "discretionary" and "non-discretionary" categories. Grapple with the items you originally thought were "indispensable" ("non-discretionary") but which can be dropped altogether. These might include newspapers and periodicals, visits to coffee shops, two cars (maybe in the UK you don't even need *one*), cable or satellite TV, entertainment, sports, luxury items such as upgrades to your TV, camera, cell phones and computers, even vacations and presents.

The Solution

Having taken the above steps, how then can you get out of debt and stay out of debt?

1. STOP SAVING

Yes, stop saving, even for such noble causes as your children's college education. *It is futile to save and borrow at the same time.* You are merely enriching the banks. Use whatever savings you do have to clear some of your debts. If not, you are borrowing at a high interest rate (say 6 percent) and saving at a lower rate (say 4 percent) and, in effect, borrowing your own money back and enriching the banks by at least 2 percent in the process! I know you are concerned about the "rainy day" or your children's education. Others will insist that it is "good" to save. Yes, it is, but *the best way to start saving is by repaying your debts.*

This also has tax advantages. Most savings plans pay interest which is taxable, whereas the interest on your debt gets no tax relief (except in the USA for house mortgages). So tax widens the gap between what the bank pays you and what you pay to the bank. In summary, use your savings to pay off your worst debt (see below). We will later look at how to cater for the "rainy day."

2. Decide Which of the Debts Listed in Your "Statement" Are Justifiable

Justifiable debts (see Chapter 1) might include the mortgage on your home, which can be seen as no debt at all because the loan is simply set off against the value of the house. In reality, you are slowly buying the house that you are renting from the bank. You own only the difference between the marketable value of the house and the mortgage, known as your "equity." If you retain your mortgage, you may want to look at refinancing it at a lower interest rate, preferably fixed over a relatively long term. If you have already paid off a substantial amount of your mortgage, you could also release some of your equity by taking a larger mortgage and paying off some of your other debts. However, *never, ever borrow more than the realizable value of the house*, and preferably only take a mortgage of 80 percent of its value. Increasing the value of the mortgage must not be done to *increase your expenditure*, only to pay off other debts which are incurring higher interest rates. You must also be careful about costs such as legal or "raising" fees or administration charges. These may cancel out any savings in interest. You may also change the type of mortgage, making it more flexible (more of this below).

3. Pay off Debts Costing You the Most Interest

Assuming that you have been able to make some cash available to pay off some of your debts, first pay off those that cost you the most interest. But there is a catch. Many debt contracts specify that you *cannot pay them off early*; if you do, you will get no reduction in interest, or may even pay a penalty. This is typical of car loan agreements. Even if you change to a cheaper or smaller car, the debt on the new car may *be loaded with the unpaid interest for the full term on the first car*. I know of people who changed their large and expensive car for a smaller one, thinking that they would save money. The monthly payments did go down, but *the term got longer*, and overall they lost a lot of money.[3]

4. Pay off Debts that Will Incur no Penalty

Do this as quickly as you can.

Working off Your Debt

What if you have no lump sum with which to repay debts? Your only hope is to work your way out of the problem as soon as you can. Here are some ideas for how to do it.

[3] See my book *Family Money Matters* for a worked example.

1. *Earn More Money*

The most obvious way is to earn more money. The options open to you include the following:

- Take on another job or do informal work for payment. Most people in the developed world work very short hours. In biblical times, a working week consisted of twelve hours a day for six days a week. Nowadays, a common working week in Western Europe is thirty-five hours, including breaks, although in the USA it is considerably longer. Only a generation ago it was forty to fifty hours per week. Holding multiple jobs is common in the USA, but in Europe (and elsewhere) it is not normal, and most employers do not allow it. However, it is usually possible to get permission if what you do neither conflicts with nor adversely affects your normal job. You may also do informal work which should draw no objections from your employer, such as turning your hobby into cash, odd-jobbing for friends and neighbors, or giving afternoon lessons to school children. You may protest that you need time for your family and so on, but look carefully at how you *actually* spend your time. You may find that you watch

Help! I'm Drowning in Debt

up to thirty-five hours of TV a week, and spend several more on your computer. Converting just your TV time into work will permit you to hold two full-time jobs *without encroaching on your current worship or family time!* The real issue is to have a more disciplined approach to the use of your time and to eliminate all unnecessary activities. I have an African friend who is not blessed with much education and never held a well-paying job, yet he owns a large house, two cars, has educated his children well, and is completely debt-free. His ingenuity in finding *extra* work has amazed me. In his younger days, for example, he collected paper and bottles for recycling, and he and his family ran a food stall in the local market on Saturday mornings. This gave them both family time and extra cash.

- If you are a husband, your wife may be able to bring in extra cash if she is not already doing so. Once again, I am not suggesting that the family should be neglected, but simply that reorganizing your life may be possible. If you believe (as I do) that it is a priority for her to be at home when the children are home, she should look for a job with hours that coincide with school hours. Alternatively, she may be able to find a job that can be done from home. Technology is making this increasingly possible. But be careful: if your wife's work causes other expenditures to increase, you may find that all her hard work is for no net gain.

- If you have teenage children, get them into paid work. It is good experience for them and can add quite a lot to the family income. Make sure that they realize that the debt problem is a *family* problem and that they enjoy both the benefits and the responsibilities of being in a family.

- You (and/or your spouse) may have to change jobs. It is not wrong to move "for money" if that represents good stewardship of your talents.

- You may discover that you can "sell' some of your vacation leave. If you enjoy generous leave (say four to six weeks), you may be able to convert some of it into cash without seriously affecting your family. Alternatively, you may be able to take on a second paid job during your vacation. If the job is to run a holiday camp, you could even have a vacation with your family at the same time! Think creatively!

2. Cut Your Expenditure

If you cannot earn more, you must make significant cuts in expenditure. Most people believe that they are living "on the edge" and that nothing can be cut. This is simply not true. Be ruthless in cutting back expenditure. Can you even afford the home you live in? If you rent, investigate renting a cheaper house. If you own your home, investigate selling it and buying a cheaper one, releasing cash with which to get out of debt and reduce your future costs. But a word of warning: I have known people who did this and the main beneficiaries were the government, the lawyers, and the realtors. Make sure that you are not tricked in the process. Remember that the agents are professionals who are keen to do a sale (or two, in this case) in order to collect their commissions. Their approach will often be to find the new home *first* and then put pressure on you to sell at a sub-optimal price in order to secure your new home. You may end up with no cash gain at all.

The most effective way to save money is to eliminate an item altogether; for example, cut out the daily visit to the coffee shop, sell one car, or terminate your cable TV. Only once you have cut out everything that you can should you look at *trimming* essential items. Here are some cost-saving ideas for essential items.

- Cut out all waste. It is estimated that over one third of all food sold in the Western world goes to waste!

- Reduce your energy bills. Ignore the pseudoscience which is propagated about not leaving cell phones on charge and other trivial savings, and focus on what really helps, that is, *on things that get hot*. This includes appliances which generate heat on standby, such as coffee makers. Reduce the temperature of your hot-water boiler and heating. Switch off heating or cooling in unused rooms, boil only enough water at a time, and cut the duration of your shower or the depth of your bath (or make it cooler). Hang your laundry on a line instead of tumble drying, and wash on "cold." Iron as little as possible. In summary, *cut heat usage*. Lighting in itself is not a large user but it tends to be on for long periods, so the obvious solution is to switch off lights when they are not needed. Refrigerators and freezers are great convenience items and reduce trips to the store. They are modest users of energy but are permanently switched on, consuming as much as 15 percent of a typical family's electricity.

Help! I'm Drowning in Debt

Set the temperature to "medium." If you have more than one, try to switch one off, especially in winter when you may not need it. Look at the technology around your home. How well is your home insulated? How accurately is the temperature in your home controlled? At a modest cost you can fit a thermostat which is programmed to keep the house at an optimum temperature at different times of the day and even days of the week. If you are about to buy a new tumble dryer, investigate the new "heat pump models," as these save up to 80 percent of the energy used. Use fluorescent lamps (including "longlife" bulbs) which save about 80 percent compared with incandescent lamps. LEDs use even less power, but they have some way to go before they produce acceptable light for general use. You may investigate solar water heating, wind- or solar-power generation, but do not spend any large sums in the forlorn hope that this will help you save money in the future: the sales pitch on these items is typically on the basis of carbon reduction, but the economics do not make sense for the typical domestic user.

▸ Cut your vacation expenses. Vacations are good

even though they are a relatively modern idea with no mention in the Bible! The key purposes of a vacation are to renew our strength, to spend significant time with our families, and to reduce stress. None of these requires an expensive trip anywhere. Your children may love just having their parents at home for a while. After my wife and I took our children on a dream vacation touring overseas, one of my children told us about a friend who was "privileged to have enjoyed a wonderful holiday." I was curious as to what such a holiday could have been. It turned out that they had gone camping. It is not the amount of money that you spend that counts, it is the quality of the interaction with your family.

- Cut your motoring costs. After your home, your car probably accounts for your largest costs and debts. If it is too late for you to stop purchasing a loan-financed car, you must minimize the impact of what may have been a foolish decision. You may investigate selling the car and clearing the debt, but I suspect that you will get no reduction on the full interest to the end of the contract, resulting in considerable loss, and the sale may not raise enough cash to clear

Help! I'm Drowning in Debt

the debt. You must therefore find other ways of reducing your costs, such as reducing car travel. Ride a bicycle, or walk more, and so on. If you have two cars, look at making do with one. Drive economically by driving smoothly. Every time you slow down or stop you discard (i.e. waste) energy which you have previously added to the car when you accelerated. Keeping to an even speed, especially between traffic lights, reduces wastage significantly. Furthermore, keep your tires at the correct pressure and do not drive around with unnecessary items in the trunk.

- Trim your household expenses. I have found that most wives are good at this so I will only make a few comments. Grow your own vegetables; this can be fun for the family and rewarding (we do this). Eliminate all luxury items, be they food, clothing or "treats." Buy clothing as seldom as is decent. My wife and I have never bothered too much about fashion, and my wife sometimes wears clothes that are over twenty years old. Cut out soda drinks, fruit juices, and bottled water. Teach your family to drink water from the tap; it will do their health

Practical Solutions

good and save money. During my student days in London, we bought the cheapest forms of all essential foods. We learned to cook the cheapest cuts of meat so well that to this day we eat them as "treats." Frugal living can be "good living" and a lot of fun.

- Investigate changing the suppliers of all your energy, telephone, TV, Internet, and mobile phones. Shop around for cheaper auto and household insurance, service agreements, and so on. Most service agreements are a waste of money and should be canceled.

A word of caution before you cut back too far on insurance. You should not drive a car at all if you cannot afford insurance to at least protect other road users. You should also maintain term life coverage on all income earners so as not to leave your heirs in even worse difficulty. Endowment policies are a combination of term insurance and savings; therefore, in line with my advice to stop saving until you have cleared most debt, try to convert these policies into pure term life coverage. In countries without a state medical service, you should also maintain health insurance.

Help! I'm Drowning in Debt

- Sell off all unnecessary "stuff." This is relatively easy on Amazon or eBay, for example.

3. Check Your Credit Cards

Credit cards are a major trap. Interest rates are exorbitant, never less than about 15 percent per annum, but often approaching 30 percent or more. Do not be fooled by interest-free periods, free credit transfers, and so on. These are recovered in an array of other fees. To make matters worse, most credit cards require only a minimum monthly payment of 5 to 10 per cent of the outstanding balance, thereby continually increasing debt. However, used properly, they can be very useful and offer certain legal protection, especially when used over the Internet. However, *never, ever use your credit card to accumulate debt, but pay it off in full every month*. The interest rates are horrific and the temptation to run up debts is very high.

4. Beware of Debt Consolidation

Debt consolidation is not a bad idea in principle. But remember that the widely advertised schemes have not been established to solve your problems but for the profit of the consolidator. First, check all the points set out above about canceling debts so that you do not end up paying double interest.

Then, assuming that all individual debts can be cleared without loss, calculate the sum of the interest payable on all of them. Compare this with the interest which will be paid on the consolidated debt. It will be surprising if the latter figure is lower than the former figure, *even though the monthly repayments may be lower*, because the period of repayment will very likely be lengthened, fooling you into believing that you are now saving money. The longer period hides the high interest charges, leaving you substantially worse off. The sales pitch is to make debts "affordable"—meaning lower monthly payments. But this is exactly the opposite of what I am recommending, which is to pay off your debts *more quickly*. A better solution—admittedly the lesser of two evils—is to release equity on your home if you can.

Here is another idea for consolidating debts. Do you have parents with capital? If so, you may be able to work out a "win-win" solution. Many older people have capital but struggle to find a reasonable interest rate to generate a living income. You may have a reasonable income but no capital. Why not borrow from your parents and pay them an interest rate mid-way between what you currently pay and what they earn? They can even save tax if you make some of what you pay them a donation. Beware, however, that you do not infringe gift or inheritance tax laws in the process. Get expert advice.

5. Arrange a Bank Overdraft

If there is such a thing as a "good" debt, it is a modest bank overdraft. The advantage of an overdraft is that any spare cash that you deposit, or any delay in paying outgoing amounts, will reduce the level of the overdraft, thereby reducing the interest charged. In this way the actual interest paid will be lower than you might expect.

6. Beware of "Zero-Interest Finance"

A word of advice on "zero-interest finance," sometimes offered on cars and consumer durables such as furniture. Remember that banks and finance houses do not give interest away; somebody has to pay for it. It may be the car manufacturer who will then try to recover the interest in the price of the car, in subsequent servicing, or in some other "hidden" cost. Check the prices out carefully for the "catch."

The fine print of these contracts will almost certainly specify that failing on a *single* payment will incur penalties and some high rate of interest on the *entire* amount from the outset to the end. Sometimes finance houses trick you into defaulting. You receive an invoice each month until you rely on it to pay each month, then they miss a month! You have been caught! If you do have such a loan, make sure that it gets paid each month, possibly using a direct debit or standing order.

7. Prepare for the "Rainy Day"

The "rainy day" problem can be solved by organizing a bank overdraft facility. Another solution is to use a flexible mortgage which allows you to repay a variable amount each month and then to withdraw any overpayment with ease. In South Africa these are called "access bonds," in the UK, "offset mortgages," "plus bonds," or "draw down mortgages," and in the USA nearly the same effect can be achieved by using a "home equity loan" linked to a mortgage. These mortgages allow you to contribute at a higher rate than is necessary but to withdraw cash if you run into the proverbial rainy day. You save interest and do not need to create a separate savings account.

Conclusion

There are many causes of debt; some are justifiable, but others are the result of succumbing to worldly thinking of instant gratification on a "Buy now, pay later" basis. This thinking may be the result of yielding to the sins of wrong priorities (not seeking first the kingdom of God), idolatry, covetousness, not being content, or lack of self-control. As such, the underlying cause of this debt is sinful and calls for repentance, which means asking for forgiveness and then *paying off all unjustified debt* as soon as possible. In many cases, the only way out of debt will be by increasing income from work and reducing expenditure.

Once you are out of debt, do the opposite, saving for some worthy causes such as your old age or to contribute toward your children's education. Even better, increase your giving to the Lord.

Personal Application Projects

Discuss/complete the following projects in a family or marital situation.

1. Get a Handle on the Facts

Draw up a Statement of Assets and Liabilities (see resources under "Where Can I Get Further Help?"), writing next to each debt the real reason for its creation using the following categories: justifiable; emergency; assistance to others; wrong priorities; covetousness; idolatry; discontentment and greed; lack of self-control.

2. Perform a Heart Checkup

(a) Read Matthew 6:19–33. In what specific ways have your priorities been wrong? What are some of the "rotten fruits" of worry, self-sufficiency, and idolatry that you see in your present situation? Who are the people who have been affected the most?

Help! I'm Drowning in Debt

(b) Read 1 Timothy 6:6–10. Write out your own definition of "contentment." In what ways is covetousness the opposite of contentment?

(c) Read Proverbs 25:28. What safeguards ("walls") can you immediately place into your life to help you cultivate self-control (e.g. don't go grocery shopping when you are hungry, leave your credit card(s) at home)?

(d) Read Proverbs 30:7–9. What do these verses teach us about contentment? Write out this passage in your own words, as your own prayer to God.

3. Make a Family Budget

(a) Prioritize your family's goals and values.

(b) List services or goods that your family can *do without completely*.

(c) List savings that can be made in essential items that cannot be removed altogether.

(d) List things that can be disposed of to pay off debt.

(e) List the skills possessed by your family. Consider your training, hobbies, etc. Can they be "sold"? If so, list the activities of the family members that will generate cash.

4. Ask Yourself a Few More Tough Questions

(a) Is it legitimate to borrow to help someone else in need? Think about how this question applies to your circumstances, whether you currently have debt or not.

(b) If you are "drowning in debt," should you stop giving to the Lord's work? Explain your reasons for your answer, and back it up with Scripture.

(c) How has God used the biblical teaching in this booklet to confront the sinful attitudes of your heart and your wrong thinking? Write out a one-page prayer to God, confessing any sins that he has convicted you of and asking for his help to be steadfast in your application of the truths you have learned.

Where Can I Get Further Help?

Publications

Edwards, Brian, *How Can I Become a Christian?* (available as a download from the DayOne Web site: www.dayonebookstore.com (USA);
www. dayone.co.uk (UK))

Temple, John, *Family Finance Matters* (Leominster: Day One, 2010). This provides details on compiling the "Statement of Assets and Liabilities" and Family Budget. Spreadsheets can be downloaded at no charge from either www.dayonebookstore.com or www.dayone.co.uk. From the home page, enter the ISBN 9781846252037 (do not use hyphens or spaces) in the search box. Once you have reached the designated page, scroll down until you come to the download link.

Web sites

USA

The Web site of Crown Financial Ministries contains information and lists books by Howard Dayton and others. Visit www.crown.org.
Also useful is:
www.daveramsey.com and www.mint.com

UK

Visit the Association of Christian Financial Advisers at www.christianfinancialadvisers.org.uk and Crown Financial Ministries UK at www.crownuk.org

OTHER COUNTRIES

Consult the Web sites given above (Crown Financial Ministries operates in eighty countries) and get a local expert to help you make any necessary changes.

Books in the *Help!* series include ...

Help! Someone I Love Has Cancer (Howard, Deborah)
ISBN 978-1-84625-217-4

Help! My Baby Has Died (Weems, Reggie)
ISBN 978-1-84625-215-0

Help! My Spouse Has Been Unfaithful (Summers, Mike)
ISBN 978-1-84625-220-4

Help! I Have Breast Cancer (Frields, Brenda)
ISBN 978-1-84625-216-7

Help! My Marriage Has Grown Cold (Thomas, Rick)
ISBN 978-1-84625-219-8

Help! He's Struggling with Pornography (Croft, Brian)
ISBN 978-1-84625-218-1

Help! My Toddler Rules the House (Tautges, Paul & Karen)
ISBN 978-1-84625-221-1

Help! Someone I Love Has Been Abused (Newheiser, Jim)
ISBN 978-1-84625-222-8

Help! I Can't Get Motivated (Embry, Adam)
ISBN 978-1-84625-248-8

Help! I'm a Single Mom (Trahan, Carol)
ISBN 978-1-84625-244-0

Help! I'm a Slave to Food (McCoy, Shannon)
ISBN 978-1-84625-242-6

Help! I'm Confused about Dating (James, Joel)
ISBN 978-1-84625-247-1

Help! I'm Drowning in Debt (Temple, Dr. John)
ISBN 978-1-84625-249-5

Help! My Teen Is Gay (Marshall, Ben)
ISBN 978-1-84625-243-3

Help! My Teen Is Rebellious (Coats, Dave & Judi)
ISBN 978-1-84625-245-7

Help! She's Struggling with Pornography (Coyle, Rachel)
ISBN 978-1-84625-246-4

(More titles in preparation)